Boats

By Heather Hammonds

Have you been on a boat?

Boats can take you
over the water.

You can see boats on the sea.

You can see boats on rivers
and lakes, too.

Two people can go
on these little boats.

It is fun to make
the boats go fast.

It is fun to make
them go slow, too.

Lots of people can go on this big boat.

This boat goes on rivers and lakes.

Some boats go very fast.

The wind pushes
this little boat along.

Big boats can go very fast, too.

The waves on the sea make the boats go up and down.

This little boat can go on a river.

The girls are making the boat go fast.

Look at the people
having a race on the river!

They are making the boats
go very fast.

It is fun to go fishing in this boat.

The boat can go on the sea.

It can go on a river
or a lake, too.

This big fishing boat
can go on the sea, too.

The men on the boat
can catch lots of fish.

Boats can pull people along the top of the water.

It is fun to be pulled along by a boat like this.

Two little boats are helping
this big boat come in
from the sea.

The little boats
are called tugboats.

It is fun to go on this big boat.

This boat has a swimming pool on it.

This big boat goes a long way out to sea.

The boat takes lots of things from place to place.

Boats on the water,
Look at them all.

Some are big,
And some are small!